Lerner SPORTS

ALL-STAR SMACKDOWN

CHRISTIAN McCAFFREY VS. LaDAINIAN TOMLINSON

WHO WOULD WIN?

SARAH ROGGIO

Lerner Publications ◆ Minneapolis

Lerner Publications Company
An imprint of Lerner Publishing Group, Inc.
241 First Avenue North
Minneapolis, MN 55401 USA

For reading levels and more information, look up this title at www.lernerbooks.com.

Main body text set in Aptifer Sans LT Pro.
Typeface provided by Linotype AG.

Editor: Anne E. Hill

Library of Congress Cataloging-in-Publication Data

Names: Roggio, Sarah, author.
Title: Christian McCaffrey vs. LaDainian Tomlinson : who would win? / Sarah Roggio.
Description: Minneapolis : Lerner Publications, 2025. | Series: All-star smackdown (Lerner sports) | Includes bibliographical references and index. | Audience: Ages 7–11 | Audience: Grades 2–3 | Summary: "Running back Christian McCaffrey is a touchdown-scoring machine for the San Francisco 49ers. LaDainian Tomlinson ranks second in NFL career rushing touchdowns. Compare and contrast their careers and then choose your rushing champion"—Provided by publisher.
Identifiers: LCCN 2024038652 (print) | LCCN 2024038653 (ebook) | ISBN 9798765668511 (library binding) | ISBN 9798765683446 (paperback) | ISBN 9798765675977 (epub)
Subjects: LCSH: McCaffrey, Christian, 1996-—Juvenile literature. | Tomlinson, LaDainian—Juvenile literature. | Running backs (Football)—Juvenile literature. | Football players—United States—Biography—Juvenile literature.
Classification: LCC GV939.M2979 R644 2025 (print) | LCC GV939.M2979 (ebook) | DDC 796.332092/2—dc23/eng/20241009

LC record available at https://lccn.loc.gov/2024038652
LC ebook record available at https://lccn.loc.gov/2024038653

Manufactured in the United States of America
1-1011545-53819-11/13/2024

TABLE OF CONTENTS

LaDainian Tomlinson

INTRODUCTION

DOUBLE TROUBLE

LaDainian Tomlinson and Christian McCaffrey are both fast running backs. These football players help teams score points.

Fast Facts

- LaDainian Tomlinson set a college football record in 1999. He had 406 rushing yards in one game.
- In 2006, Tomlinson set an NFL record. He had 31 touchdowns in one season.
- Christian McCaffrey set a college football record in 2015. He had 3,864 all-purpose yards in one season.
- In 2023, McCaffrey set a San Francisco 49ers record. He had 24 touchdowns in one season.

Running backs must be able to run with the football. But Tomlinson and McCaffrey are also great at catching the ball. These skills make them double trouble on the field.

In 2005, Tomlinson was playing for the National Football League (NFL)'s San Diego Chargers. It was the first quarter against the Oakland Raiders. Chargers quarterback Drew Brees threw the ball to a wide-open Tomlinson. He easily ran the ball in for a touchdown. Later in the first quarter, Tomlinson rushed for a second touchdown.

Christian McCaffrey

In the second quarter, Brees handed Tomlinson the ball. Then Tomlinson made a surprise pass to Justin Peelle for a touchdown. With this play, Tomlinson did something few NFL players do. He ran, threw, and passed for a touchdown all in one game! He was only the seventh player in NFL history to do this.

McCaffrey joined this short list 17 years later. In 2022, McCaffrey was playing for the San Francisco 49ers. It was the second quarter against the Los Angeles Rams. McCaffrey threw a 34-yard pass to Brandon Aiyuk for a touchdown.

Tomlinson carries the ball in a game against the Oakland Raiders on October 14, 2007.

In the third quarter, McCaffrey caught a touchdown pass. And in the fourth quarter, McCaffrey ran for a 1-yard touchdown. He ran, threw, and passed for a touchdown all in one game. He was the first NFL player since Tomlinson to do this.

Both Tomlinson and McCaffrey are powerhouse players. But which one is the best? Read on to decide who wins this smackdown!

McCaffrey runs the ball in a December 2023 game versus the Arizona Cardinals.

CHAPTER 1

Tomlinson (center) sprints down the field in a TCU game against Fresno State in 2000.

BORN TO RUN

LaDainian Tomlinson and Christian McCaffrey both grew up loving football. LaDainian was born on June 23, 1979. He grew up in Texas. He held his first football at just four years old. He knew then he wanted to play. By the age of six, he had his sights set on the NFL. When he was 12, LaDainian went to a football camp where he got to meet star NFL running back Emmitt Smith.

LaDainian played running back in high school. He played for University High School in Waco, Texas. He could run far and fast. He had 2,554 rushing yards in one season. This was a Waco record. Texas Christian University (TCU) asked him to play for their team.

Tomlinson set a record for rushing yards at Texas Christian University.

At TCU, Tomlinson led the US in rushing yards in 1999 and 2000. In 2001, his NFL dream came true. The San Diego Chargers picked him fifth overall in the NFL draft. In his first year as a pro, he rushed for 1,236 yards.

Christian McCaffrey was born on June 7, 1996. He grew up in Colorado. He started playing football when he was seven. His father, Ed, and his older brother, Max, both played in the NFL. When Christian was a teenager, his father started a football camp for children with Down syndrome. Christian loved to help teach football to kids at the camp.

Christian (left) and his older brother, Max, played together at Valor Christian High School in Colorado.

As a high school running back, Christian (center) was fast on the field.

Christian was a running back in high school. He played for Valor Christian in Highlands Ranch, Colorado. Like Tomlinson, he was incredibly fast. Christian's father pushed him to play his best. Christian had 5,340 total rushing yards in high school.

CONSIDER THIS

Kyle Shanahan is the head coach of the San Francisco 49ers. The 49ers traded for McCaffrey during the 2022 season. In the 1990s, when Shanahan was a teenager, he used to babysit McCaffrey.

McCaffrey went on to play at Stanford University. He set an NCAA record his second year at Stanford. He had 3,864 all-purpose yards in one season. All-purpose yards include rushing, receiving, and kick-return yards. After college, the Carolina Panthers picked him eighth overall in the 2017 NFL draft.

McCaffrey set an NCAA record while playing at Stanford University.

McCaffrey was awarded the Offensive Player of the Game Award at the Rose Bowl on January 1, 2016.

CHAPTER 2

Tomlinson (center) runs past Northwestern's Pete Konopka during a September 2000 game.

GAME CHANGERS

Tomlinson and McCaffrey are both skilled at gaining yards for their teams. Running backs gain most of their yards on rushing plays. They take the ball from the quarterback and run with it. But Tomlinson and McCaffrey are also skilled receivers. They can gain a lot of yards by catching passes. They have impressive stats in both rushing and receiving yards.

TCU fans watched Tomlinson race past the other teams' defenses. In 1999, he set an NCAA record. He had 406 rushing yards in one game. He had 287 yards in the second half of this game. Tomlinson graduated from TCU with 5,263 total rushing yards. He also scored 54 touchdowns.

Tomlinson (left) speaks with SiriusXM host Steve Torre during the Super Bowl on January 29, 2020.

Working as an NFL network analyst, Tomlinson comments on a game in December 2016.

In the NFL, Tomlinson worked to improve his pass catching. He made 624 career catches for 4,772 receiving yards. He also had 17 total touchdown receptions. Tomlinson retired from the NFL in 2012. Then he worked for 10 years as a TV football analyst.

CONSIDER THIS

In 2015, the Chargers retired Tomlinson's jersey number to honor his football skills. This means no other Chargers player can wear Tomlinson's number 21 jersey.

McCaffrey could run and catch well before he reached the NFL. Stanford fans watched him make fast turns at top speed with the ball. He could catch the ball with one hand. In 2015, he gained 369 all-purpose yards in one game.

McCaffrey worked hard to keep improving his skills. He graduated from Stanford with 3,922 total rushing yards. He also made 99 catches for 1,206 receiving yards. He had 10 total touchdown receptions as well.

McCaffrey rushes down the field in a game against the Washington Huskies in September 2016.

McCaffrey showed off his rushing and receiving skills early in his NFL career. He ran for a 56-yard touchdown in his first year in the NFL. In 2019, he had 1,000 rushing yards for the Panthers. He also had 1,000 receiving yards. He was the third NFL player in history to do both in one season.

Through his first seven NFL seasons, McCaffrey had a total of 509 catches for 4,320 receiving yards. He also had 29 touchdown receptions.

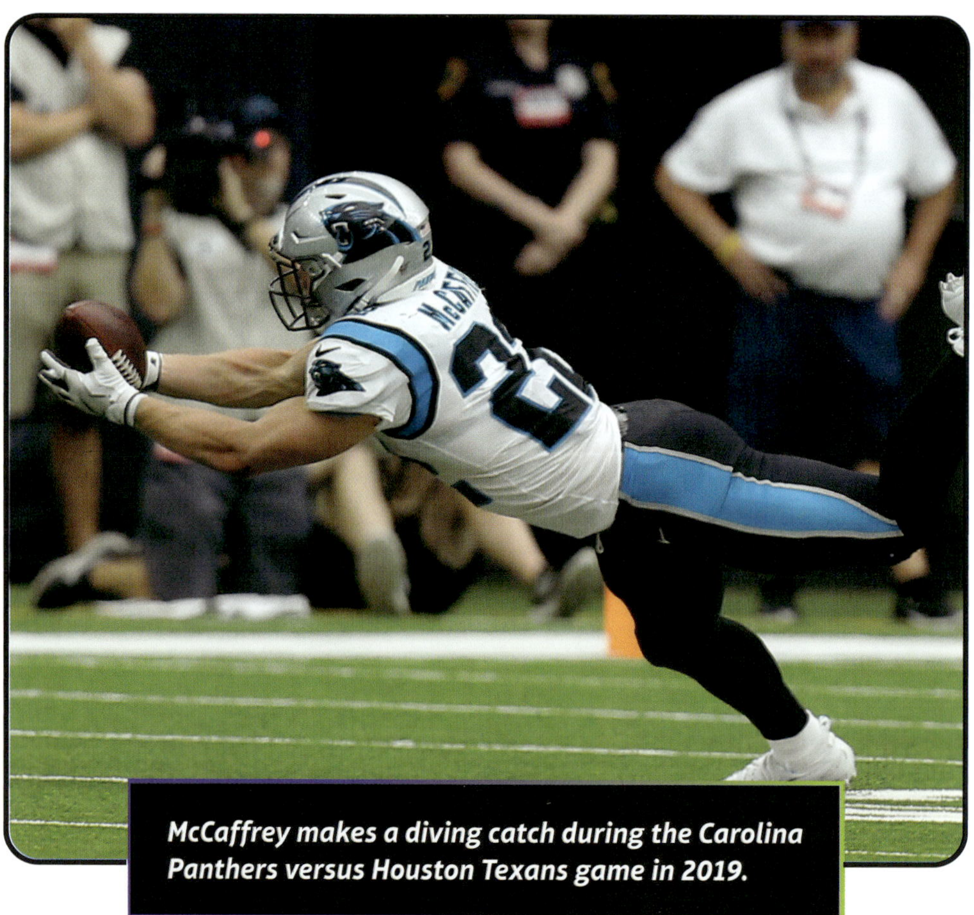

McCaffrey makes a diving catch during the Carolina Panthers versus Houston Texans game in 2019.

McCaffrey scores a touchdown by leaping over the head of Tre Herndon of the Jacksonville Jaguars.

CHAPTER 3

Tomlinson leaps into the end zone for his third touchdown of the day during a 2006 game against the 49ers.

STAR RUNNING BACKS

Fans love to watch both Tomlinson and McCaffrey on the field. They have made exciting plays. They have caught tricky passes. Both have broken free from tackles. They have been known to sneak past defenses and zoom down the field to score touchdowns.

Tomlinson is 5 feet 10 (1.7 m). He was considered small for a running back. But he was speedy. In college, he ran a 40-yard dash in 4.39 seconds. His speed helped TCU win two college bowl games. In 2000, Tomlinson earned the Doak Walker Award. This award honors the top college running back in the nation.

In the NFL, Tomlinson played nine years with the Chargers. Then he played two years with the New York Jets. He never won a Super Bowl. But he led the Chargers to five winning seasons. In 2006, he set an NFL record of 31 touchdowns in one season. That year he was named the NFL's Most Valuable Player.

Tomlinson (left) and Drew Brees were Walter Payton Man of the Year cowinners in 2007.

CONSIDER THIS

Tomlinson has an amazing 145 rushing touchdowns in his career. This is second only to the legendary Emmitt Smith with a whopping 164. McCaffrey has 52 rushing touchdowns as of the end of the 2023 NFL season.

McCaffrey is 1 inch (2.5 cm) taller than Tomlinson. McCaffrey was also fast in college. He ran a 40-yard dash in 4.48 seconds. His speed and football skills helped Stanford win three college bowl games. He was the first player in Rose Bowl history with 100 yards rushing and 100 receiving yards. McCaffrey was a two-time finalist for the Doak Walker Award.

McCaffrey runs the ball for the Carolina Panthers in a game against the Tampa Bay Buccaneers in November 2018.

McCaffrey celebrates a touchdown at the 2024 Super Bowl against the Kansas City Chiefs.

McCaffrey played five full seasons with the Panthers. After six games in 2022, the team traded him to the 49ers. He has led the 49ers to two winning seasons.

In 2024, they made it to the Super Bowl. McCaffrey had 80 rushing and 80 receiving yards in the big game. The 49ers lost to the Kansas City Chiefs. But McCaffrey finished 2024 as the top NFL rusher with 1,459 yards.

CHAPTER 4

McCaffrey catches a pass during a practice for the 2023 NFL Pro Bowl.

AND THE WINNER IS

It can be hard to compare two great players who played at different times. Picking a winner is not easy. It is a personal choice. Not everyone will agree, and that's okay.

In February 2017, Tomlinson learned he would join the Pro Football Hall of Fame. That same year, McCaffrey began his

NFL career. Neither player has won a Super Bowl. But both players are all-time great running backs.

Coaches, players, and fans have voted both McCaffrey and Tomlinson into several Pro Bowls. In 2024, McCaffrey was named NFL Offensive Player of the Year. With McCaffrey in the spotlight, some fans wonder if he is better than past players such as Tomlinson.

McCaffrey fans point to his 6,185 rushing yards and 82 total touchdowns in his first seven NFL seasons. In 2019, he broke Tomlinson's receiving record. He had 246 receptions in his first three years in the NFL. Tomlinson had 238 receptions in his first three years. In 2023, McCaffrey set a San Francisco 49ers record with 24 touchdowns in one season.

McCaffrey took home the Offensive Player of the Year Award in 2024.

Tomlinson (left) unveils his NFL Hall of Fame bust on August 5, 2017.

But Tomlinson fans can point to other stats. He beats McCaffrey with a career total of 13,684 rushing yards. He also has a total of 162 touchdowns. This is the third-highest total in NFL history. Tomlinson played in 10 playoff games. McCaffrey has played in only seven playoff games.

Tomlinson's amazing stats make him the winner of this smackdown. But McCaffrey is still playing and getting better. He might pass Tomlinson's stats in the future. He could even get a Super Bowl win one day.

Both Tomlinson and McCaffrey are superstar running backs. When choosing a winner, there is no right or wrong answer. People have different opinions about what makes a running back great. Who do you think is best? Think about their stats and make your own choice!

Tomlinson at the 2007 NFL Pro Bowl

SMACKDOWN BREAKDOWN

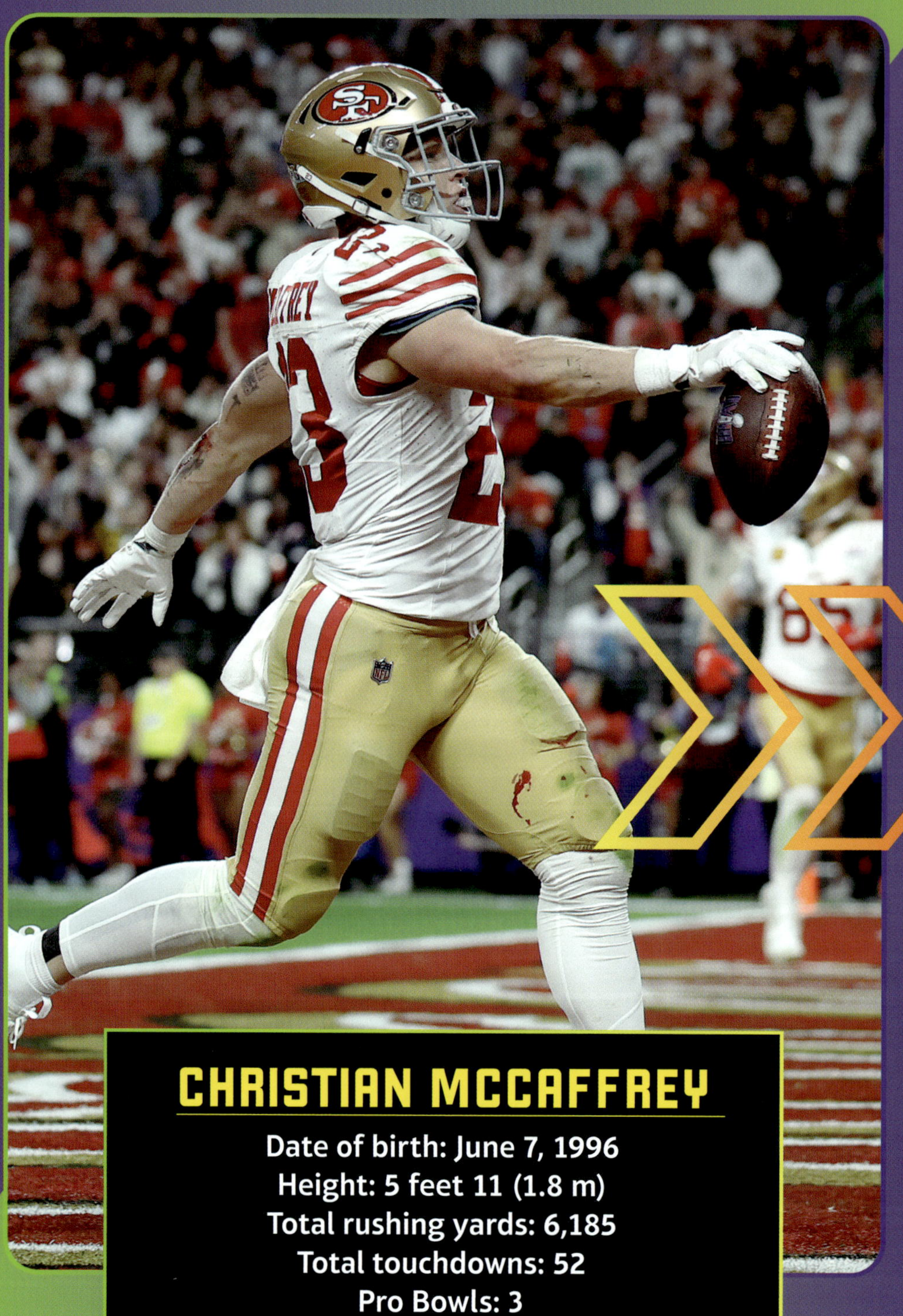

CHRISTIAN MCCAFFREY

Date of birth: June 7, 1996
Height: 5 feet 11 (1.8 m)
Total rushing yards: 6,185
Total touchdowns: 52
Pro Bowls: 3

Stats are accurate through the 2023 NFL regular season.

LADAINIAN TOMLINSON

Date of birth: June 23, 1979
Height: 5 feet 10 (1.8 m)
Total rushing yards: 13,684
Total touchdowns: 162
Pro Bowls: 5

GLOSSARY

bowl game: a game played at the end of the college football season

Down syndrome: a condition that can cause health issues and trouble with learning

draft: when teams take turns choosing new players

football analyst: someone who provides information about football plays, players, and teams

NCAA: National Collegiate Athletic Association, the group that sets rules for college sports

Pro Bowl: the NFL's all-star game

receiving yard: a yard gained in a passing play

reception: the catching of a forward pass

rushing yard: a yard gained in a running play

Super Bowl: the NFL's final game to determine the league champion

LEARN MORE

Britannica Kids: San Francisco 49ers
https://kids.britannica.com/students/article/San-Francisco-49ers/571024

Christian McCaffrey Foundation
https://christianmccaffreyfoundation.org

Greenberg, Keith Elliot. *Christian McCaffrey*. Minneapolis: Lerner Publications, 2022.

Hill, Christina. *Inside the San Francisco 49ers*. Minneapolis: Lerner Publications, 2023.

Pro Football Hall of Fame: LaDainian Tomlinson
https://www.profootballhof.com/players/ladainian-tomlinson/

Tustison, Matt. *Awesome NFL Records*. Mankato, MN: Black Rabbit Books, 2025.

INDEX

PHOTO ACKNOWLEDGMENTS

Owen C. Shaw/Getty Images, p. 4; Lachlan Cunningham/Getty Images, p. 5; Focus on Sport/Getty Images, pp. 6, 27, 29; Norm Hall/Getty Images, p. 7; Ronald Martinez/Getty Images, pp. 8, 14; John W. McDonough/Sports Illustrated via Getty Images, p. 9; Karl Gehring/The Denver Post via Getty Images, pp. 10, 11; Thearon W. Henderson/Getty Images, p. 12; Harry How/Getty Images, p. 13; Cindy Ord/Getty Images for SiriusXM, p. 15; Ken Murray/Icon Sportswire via Getty Images, p. 16; Otto Greule Jr/Getty Images, p. 17; Bob Levey/Getty Images, p. 18; Jacob Kupferman/Getty Images, p. 19; Robert B. Stanton/NFLPhotoLibrary, p. 20; Donald Miralle/Getty Images, p. 21; Streeter Lecka/Getty Images, p. 22; Ryan Kang/Getty Images, p. 23; AP Photo/Michael Owens, p. 24; Perry Knotts/Getty Images, p. 25; Paul Moseley/Fort Worth Star-Telegram/Tribune News Service via Getty Images, p. 26; Ezra Shaw/Getty Images, p. 28.

Cover photos: AP Photo/Scot Tucker (McCaffrey); AP Photo/Denis Poroy (Tomlinson).